STARTING HERE STARTING NOW

A
NEW MUSICAL REVUE
BY
RICHARD   DAVID
MALTBY, JR.   SHIRE

T0087314

CONTENTS

Edited by Frank Metis

RICHARD MALTBY, JR. & DAVID SHIRE

Martin Gottfried, N.Y. Post Drama Critic, wrote of Maltby and Shire and STARTING HERE, STARTING NOW:

> "This is a team of formidable talent and theatrical flair, superior to most and then some. We're presented with songs that are musically and lyrically sophisticated; . . . songs that present the feel and the quality of the Broadway musical theatre at full strength."

Richard Maltby, Jr. and David Shire began their long collaboration by writing two musicals presented at Yale University while they were still undergraduates. Professionally, they contributed scores to the musicals THE SAP OF LIFE, produced Off-Broadway in New York, HOW DO YOU DO, I LOVE YOU, which starred Phyllis Newman, and LOVE MATCH, which was presented at the Ahmanson Theatre in Los Angeles. Some material from these scores is included in STARTING HERE, STARTING NOW. They have contributed material to GRAHAM CRACKERS, NEW FACES OF 1968 and THAT WAS THE WEEK THAT WAS, and their songs have been recorded by many top artists including Barbra Streisand, who has recorded "AUTUMN", "STARTING HERE, STARTING NOW", and "WHAT ABOUT TODAY?" among others.

When not working together, both Maltby and Shire have pursued extremely successful careers on their own. Maltby won a Tony Award in 1978 for his direction of AIN'T MISBEHAVIN', a show which he also conceived and which won the Tony as Best Musical of 1978. Previously he directed successful productions of LONG DAY'S JOURNEY INTO NIGHT, THE GLASS MENAGERIE, and STREET SONGS, all starring Geraldine Fitzgerald, and he conceived and directed the original production of STARTING HERE, STARTING NOW. In his spare time, Maltby has written devilish crossword puzzles for New York Magazine and Harper's.

David Shire has achieved a reputation as one of the finest contemporary film composers. His numerous movie scores include those for NORMA RAE, THE CONVERSATION, ALL THE PRESIDENT'S MEN, THE TAKING OF PELHAM 1-2-3, FAREWELL, MY LOVELY, THE HINDENBERG and adaptation and additional music for SATURDAY NIGHT FEVER, and he has twice been nominated for Emmys for his extensive television work. His songs have been recorded by such artists as Melissa Manchester, Judy Collins, Jennifer Warnes, Debby Boone, Billy Preston, and Arthur Fiedler, and he won two Grammys for his contributions to the SATURDAY NIGHT FEVER album.

On the opening of STARTING HERE, STARTING NOW, Edwin Wilson of the Wall Street Journal observed:

> "Probably no other songwriters alive could provide a full evening of songs so generally unfamiliar and yet so delightful as these".

STARTING HERE, STARTING NOW

Lyrics by
RICHARD MALTBY, Jr.

Music by
DAVID SHIRE

A LITTLE BIT OFF

Lyrics by
RICHARD MALTBY, Jr.

Music by
DAVID SHIRE

Moderately bright, with an "old time" feel

I THINK I MAY WANT TO REMEMBER TODAY

Lyrics by
RICHARD MALTBY, Jr.

Music by
DAVID SHIRE

write   all   this   down   in   my   book._____ For
to - tal - ly   beau - ti - ful   man._____ And

oh,_____

poco a poco cresc.

_____ I   Think   I   May   Want   To   Re -

f

1.

mem - ber_____ To - day._____

14

Tap - er - ing down to his hips.

When we met as chil - dren,

He was skin and bone. Oh,

Al bert...

My, how you've grown! As a mat- ter of course, I should like to con - fess That I hear a re - mark - a - ble sound. To be per - fect - ly hon - est, I think it's no less Than my

to - ber._____ I know I shall want to re-

mem - ber_____ to-

day!_____

CROSSWORD PUZZLE

Lyrics by
RICHARD MALTBY, Jr.

Music by
DAVID SHIRE

20

blot." He'd say, "Af - ghan - i no - mad," _____

_____ And I'd say, "It's a Kurd." I'd let him hold the

pen - cil. _____ He could write in the word. And when

a little slower   *poco rit.*

Freely

he was hav-ing trou-ble spell-ing "Tryst;" *(Spoken):* T - R - *Y* - S - T; *(Sung):* I showed him, how I showed him...

(colla voce)   *f broadly*   *mp*

word mean - ing…Why should it hap - pen to us? There was nev - er a mo - ment's
word mean - ing Phi Be - ta Kap - pa, that's me. I'm as bright as a girl can

doubt. All at once Heck - y's jump - ing and scream - ing and yell - ing, I tell you, the
be. So bright some - one else who could not tell a fig from a frig - ate is

al Coda (Spoken):

four - let - ter words that came "Out, Pre - fix," that means "Pro,"
off with my Heck - y at…

(Sung):

P - R - O. Bo - de - o - do. Starts you feel - ing as if hav - ing

brains or in - tel - li - gence was one of the world's worst crimes; _____ And the

sen - tence is do - ing the cross - word puz - zle in the Sun - day...

♩=♩. **With a Viennese lilt**

All the times Heck - y'd tell me: _____ "You shut

up, this *I'll* get! Sev - en blanks mean - ing

'air - hole,'_____ It's 'fis - tu - la' I bet."

I'd say, "No," he'd say, "Don't tell me;

(Spoken): *(Sung):*

it's 'tu - bu - lus'... 'Tu - bu - lae!'"_____

f

decresc.

I'd say, "Heck - y, it's 'chim - ney!'"_____

mp *rall.*

AUTUMN

Lyrics by
RICHARD MALTBY, Jr.

Music by
DAVID SHIRE

I DON'T REMEMBER CHRISTMAS

Lyrics by
RICHARD MALTBY, Jr.

Music by
DAVID SHIRE

Moderately (in 2) - Hard Jazz Samba

I HEAR BELLS

Lyrics by
RICHARD MALTBY, Jr.

Music by
DAVID SHIRE

Moderato (rhythmically)

mp

(with pedal)

I Hear Bells _____ in the sum - mer night,
Call me mad, _____ well, of course you will.

mp

Dis - tant bells that no one hears.
Put me un - der no lock and key.

I hear moon - light
I'll hear mu - sic

mf

soft - ly chim - ing, And the clang of i - vy climb - ing.
where I'm room - ing, Like the bong of ro - ses bloom - ing.

42

TRAVEL

Lyrics by
RICHARD MALTBY, Jr.

Music by
DAVID SHIRE

WATCHING THE BIG PARADE GO BY

Lyrics by
RICHARD MALTBY, Jr.

Music by
DAVID SHIRE

Do - in' their drill, prov - in' their skill, thrill - in' the fel - low who's watch-in' from up in a

tree: _____

Me.

Af - ter the crowd is gone, _____ Of - ten I lin - ger on, _____

Think a-bout me, _____ There's got-ta be me! _____

_____ If I like it, I will

cheer it, Cheer it loud and let 'em hear it. How can there be a pa-

rade with-out a crowd? _____ Proud - ly the mu - sic

FLAIR

Lyrics by
RICHARD MALTBY, Jr.

Music by
DAVID SHIRE

Fast Vaudeville Tempo (in 2)

Hey there, fans, ___ here to say, ___ Per-

haps you'd like to know how I get through the day. ___

Hard work, dull work, play-ing the clown, ___ If

WHAT ABOUT TODAY?

Music and Lyrics by
DAVID SHIRE

76

ONE STEP

Lyrics by
RICHARD MALTBY, Jr.

Music by
DAVID SHIRE

80

BARBARA

Lyrics by
RICHARD MALTBY, Jr.

Music by
DAVID SHIRE

SONG OF ME

Lyrics by
RICHARD MALTBY, Jr.

Music by
DAVID SHIRE

Moderately (not too slowly) with rubato

92

TODAY IS THE FIRST DAY OF THE REST OF MY LIFE

Lyrics by
RICHARD MALTBY, Jr.

Music by
DAVID SHIRE

94

DAVID SHIRE (Composer) previously collaborated with Richard Maltby, Jr. on the Off-Broadway revue *Starting Here, Starting Now,* which has had over 250 productions worldwide since its New York run. He composed the songs and incidental music for Joseph Papp's New York Shakespeare Festival production of *As You Like It* and the original production of Peter Ustinov's *The Unknown Soldier And His Wife.* He has been nominated twice for Academy Awards and won the Oscar in 1980 for *It Goes Like It Goes* from *Norma Rae.* His many film scores include *All The President's Men, The Conversation, The Taking Of Pelham 1-2-3 and Farewell, My Lovely;* and his television scores have earned him two Emmy nominations. His songs have been recorded by Barbra Streisand, Melissa Manchester, Maureen McGovern, Judy Collins, Jennifer Warnes, Debbie Boone, Laura Branigan and Johnny Mathis, among many others, and "With You I'm Born Again", recorded by Billy Preston and Syreeta, was an international hit. He has received a Grammy nomination for the cast album of *Starting Here, Starting Now,* and two Grammy Awards for his contributions as both a composer and producer to the *Saturday Night Fever* album. He is married to actress Didi Conn and is the father of Matthew Shire.

RICHARD MALTBY, JR. (Director/Lyricist) won the 1978 Tony Award as best director of a musical for conceiving and directing *Ain't Misbehavin'* which also won the Tony Award, the New York Drama Critics' Circle Award, the Outer Critics Circle Award, the Drama Desk Award and an Obie as best musical of 1978. The RCA Original Cast Album won a Grammy in 1979. He directed and wrote the lyrics for the 1977 Off-Broadway musical hit *Starting Here, Starting Now,* with music by David Shire. The RCA Original Cast Album was nominated for a Grammy. Mr. Maltby directed the record-breaking Philadelphia Drama Guild production of *Long Days Journey Into Night* and *The Glass Menagerie,* both starring Geraldine Fitzgerald, for whom he also directed a highly successful one-woman show called *Street Songs.* With Ms. Fitzgerald and director Arvin Brown he wrote the musical version of *Juno And The Peacock,* with a score by Marc Blitzstein produced at the Long Wharf Theatre in New Haven and at the Williamstown Theatre Festival. He has a long term association with the Manhattan Theatre Club where he directed the musical *Livin' Dolls.* The son of the well-known orchestra leader, Maltby also contributes devilish crossword puzzles to Harper's Magazine. He is the father of two sons, Nicholas and David.